FOR THE QUIET BLACK GIRL:
TRYING TO FIND HER VOICE IN A PREDOMINATELY WHITE SPACE

Valentina,
    Always speak your
truth. You are important.
Thank you for asking
all of your amazing
questions. ♡ Aundrea Tabbs-Smith

BY

AUNDREA TABBS-SMITH

ISBN: 978-0-9995381-0-4 (sc)
ISBN: 978-0-9995381-1-1(e)

Editor: Rhonda A. Gordon
Publisher: P31 Publishing, LLC

For more information, please visit www.spithoney.com
Instagram: spit_honey

I dedicate this book to my children. May you always know that you are beautiful, intelligent human beings whose voices have the power to change the world.

I love you.

Table of Contents

Preface vii

Chapter 1: STILL ASLEEP 1

Chapter 2: ASSUMPTIONS 5

Chapter 3: PEN PALS AND APPLE SAUCE 9

Chapter 4: "DO YOU WANT TO BE WHITE?" 11

Chapter 5: "SHINE MY SHOES, SLAVE GIRL" 13

Chapter 6: LISPTICK AND LIES 17

Chapter 7: JUST A SKINNY BLACK GIRL 19

Chapter 8: DÉJÀ VU 23

Chapter 9: "MAYBE NEXT TIME" 25

Chapter 10: IS IT WORTH IT? 27

Chapter 11: AWAKE 29

Epilogue: SPEAK YOUR TRUTH 33

PREFACE

Black women in this country have endured a lot. I feel that we are expected to wear so many hats. It is assumed that we are strong and outspoken at all times. It is also assumed that we are unintelligent, ugly human beings who do not deserve to be in the same space as white people. Our efforts and qualifications are often overlooked because some people choose to only see the dark skin that adorns our bodies and they associate it with being unworthy; unworthy of respect, a job, a decent income, and anything else that could potentially build us up and move us in a positive direction.

Our society pushes and pulls us in so many directions. I am told one minute that I am too quiet and the next that I have a "black girl attitude." Associates and colleagues tell us that we "speak so well" or ask, "What did you do to your hair?" after we cut or style it a certain way. People watch reality TV and think that's how all black women act. They think we are one-dimensional. We have no layers. We can't cry, get mad, have an opinion (or not have an opinion), or work at certain establishments without being judged and criticized.

Most people do not realize how much black women have to

endure. Although we may not all experience the same exact situations, our own journeys and the experiences of the other black women in our lives, have helped shape us. Our demeanor, our ability to cope, our flexibility, our dialect, our style, our outlook on life.... are all affected by the "black girl experience." The color of our skin and our gender has pre-determined our existence.

We are resilient. However, at times, our resilience seems to overshadow the fact that we are human.

CHAPTER 1

STILL ASLEEP

When you look at me, there is no doubt that I am a black woman; however, while I was growing up, my blackness, or lack thereof, was a constant topic of conversation. I grew up in Westchester County, New York. My family moved to Westchester from Detroit, Michigan when I was one and a half years old. My dad had a position at IBM and was asked to move to the area. Still to this day I do not understand how my parents left their family and friends behind in Michigan. That's a twelve hour drive away from their comfort zone. I know it was not an easy decision. We lived in a hotel while we waited for the family whose house we were purchasing to move out. I do not remember anything about living the hotel life, but every now and then I drive by where we used to stay and create scenarios in my mind of us being there. I picture me attempting to walk down the hallway and my dad following closely behind, ready to catch my fall. I picture us sitting in the room eating hotel food or takeout from somewhere. Me, on my mom's lap, her attempting to feed me without making a mess, and my dad sitting at one of the desks, prepared to hand my mom a napkin if needed.

We lived in the hotel for two weeks, and we moved into my childhood home during the summer of 1984. We lived in a great neighborhood. It was quiet and welcoming. Everyone played with one another. It was almost like what you see in the movies, kids running from house to house asking, "Can Allen come out and play?" Sleepovers, bike rides through our elderly neighbor's yard (almost giving her a heart attack), walking down to the corner store, and visits from "Joe the Ice Cream Man" are just some of the memories I have growing up on Trenton Avenue.

Actually, the best part of living on my street were the block parties. Our street would get blocked off, tables would be set up, and folks would bring dishes from all around the world. I remember one of my neighbors made the BEST quiche from scratch. I would hover over her until she pulled off the aluminum foil. I probably had three or four pieces in one sitting. Then we would ride our bikes in the street, play tag, and hide-and-go-seek until it got dark. On this night, and this night only, when the street lights came on we were allowed to stay outside. I truly miss those times. Even to this day I yearn to live on a block like that. I don't know if they exist anymore.

It was the sense of community that made me feel at ease. We literally would ask each other for eggs and sugar. We were that type of neighborhood. I did not worry. I knew my neighbors would have my back in any situation. One day while riding my bike on our street (I was about nine years old), I either forgot to apply the brakes, or they malfunctioned. The next thing I knew, I was speeding down the hill and ran into a neighbor's fence. Thank God there wasn't a car coming because I would've been hit. The neighbor, an elderly gentleman, heard my screams and cries and tried to comfort me in Portuguese. I did not know him well, but I remember he would bring custard tarts to the block parties and gather all the kids on the block and tell us funny stories. This man carried me up the hill and brought me to my front door. "Oh, my baby!" my mom yelled when she opened the door. I can still hear her voice as if it were yesterday. My mom asked him to come in and rest, but he bashfully declined and headed back down the hill. I was so happy to be home and immediately turned into a three year old while explaining to my mom what happened. As I told her the story, she grabbed me some ice and Band-Aids and patched me up wherever she saw a bruise or a cut. No broken bones, and I was probably more dramatic than I needed to be, but that man is just an example of what made my neighborhood so great.

CHAPTER 2

ASSUMPTIONS

My parents still live on Trenton Avenue. They have been married for thirty-seven years. Both of them have always taught my sister and me that we had to work hard to get results. They showed us the importance of loving ourselves and being resilient. It was their ability to demonstrate good character that allowed me to develop my own. I did not get a lot of lectures. I was not yelled at. My mom and dad lived their lives in such a way that I wanted to emulate their values and principles. What's funny is they both have very different personalities. My mom is very composed; I rarely see anything or anyone stress her out. She trusts God with EVERYTHING, and has the ability to calmly tell someone about him or herself. My dad can talk to anyone. I remember standing next to him for what felt like hours as he spoke to random people in a store. He loves to help other people and even created his own organization for girls in Harlem to give them the opportunity to experience playing for the Amateur Athletic Union (AAU) basketball. He is all about being your best self — presenting yourself well and working hard. He is also known to throw out a cuss word or two if someone cuts him off while driving. My parents met at Michigan State. My dad, the quiet bookworm, and my mom, the outgoing free spirit, met at a dorm party in Wilson Hall. Their opposing dispositions connected, got married, and created two daughters.

Church has always been something that connected my family. My dad did not attend church with us every Sunday (he prefers to have his time with God alone and without anyone and everyone asking him a thousand questions, which can sometimes happen at black churches), but when my sister, Candace, and I were in a play, he was always in the audience – camcorder in hand. The three of us were members of a Baptist church. I was in the church orchestra, youth and young adult ministries, attended Sunday school, and went to Vacation Bible School. I did all of these things, all while being the "quiet kid." Unfortunately, assumptions were made about me, even in church. I remember sitting in one of my Sunday school classes when I was about ten or eleven years old, and before class officially started some of the kids were talking about extracurricular activities. One boy mentioned he had basketball practice every day after school. He then turned to me and said, "Aundrea, how often does your team practice?" and before I even had a chance to answer, the teacher jumped in and said, "Aundrea, you don't play basketball. I am sure you're into dance or art or something on that order."

The boy shook his head and said, "No, she plays. I've watched her. She's good." The teacher was dumbfounded. I am sure she wondered how this scrawny kid who barely talks could be any good at playing ball. "Really? I don't believe it," she replied.

I loved playing ball. I became another person on the court. It was almost like my "Sasha Fierce" moment. I was loud, aggressive, and played "D" like my life depended on it. Basketball was my outlet. It allowed me to release a side of me that I was not sure how to reveal when not on the court. I played in school, for recreational leagues, and AAU. My dad would drive me down to the city to play on a team in Harlem. Those girls were so strong. They unknowingly taught me a lot about not only physical strength, but mental strength, as well. I know at the time I complained to my dad that the girls were hard on me and I did not want to play with them anymore, but I'm glad that he pushed me to keep going. I played in Slam Jam tournaments and Nike leagues. I even played at Rucker Park. Rucker Park is the breeding grounds of some of the greatest professional basketball players to have ever played basketball. Today, Rucker Park holds many tournaments with the main focus to help raise money for less fortunate children go to college.

Those were really great times in my life, and I am so grateful for my dad for that experience.

CHAPTER 3

PEN PALS AND APPLE SAUCE

I attended one of the local public schools during my grade school years, and although I was reserved, I had good friends and truly enjoyed my time in school. I remember all of my grade school teachers' names. I think that's one of the reasons why I decided to go into the teaching profession. Teachers have such an immense power over the students that enter their classrooms. A teacher's impact can be one that turns a child away from learning or draws them in to all that school can offer. The memories that are created during a child's grade school years stay with them for the rest of their lives. I don't think many of us realize the moments during that time in our lives help develop us into who we are as adults.

When I was in second grade my teacher paired us up with college student pen pals. My pen pal's name was Jillian and I thought she was the most amazing person in the world. Her handwriting was perfect. I tried to emulate it when I wrote my letters to her, but that did not pan out too well. I am surprised she could even respond to the questions I had in my letters. After several letters had been mailed back and forth, my teacher arranged for our pen pals to visit us at school. I felt like I was about to meet a celebrity. My palms started to sweat and I think I may have started hyperventilating (so dramatic). I could not wipe the grin off my face. I don't think I said a word the entire time she was in the classroom. I remember nothing from our conversation, but she gave me a card before she left and we took a picture together. I'm pretty sure it's still in my parents' house somewhere.

When I was in the fourth grade my teacher looped with us to fifth grade. I remember a feeling of pure joy when I found out. Mrs. Epstein had such a great classroom presence. She truly made learning fun. We played Oregon Trail during social studies and engaged in several group projects without feeling like we were about to be tortured for the next forty-five minutes. I distinctly remember her bringing in her "famous" potato pancakes. She taught us that the proper way to eat them were with a little bit of applesauce or sour cream. The applesauce was my favorite. It is fond memories like these that I cherish from elementary school. However, it was also during this time that my eyes were opened to how other black children perceived me.

CHAPTER 4

"DO YOU WANT TO BE WHITE?"

I had friends from diverse backgrounds. There were a solid number of black and brown kids at the school; however, I do not believe we were the majority. I got to school early and left school late. Both of my parents worked, so that's what had to be done. Like many public schools, the after school program took place in the cafeteria. I remember getting into an argument with one of the boys there. He was trying to convince me that God wasn't real. I definitely used my voice then. I think I had to "take a break" for yelling at him.

Most of the friends I became closest to were white. I did not think anything of it until one day another black student spotted me in the hallway and asked me if I wanted to be white. I was walking alone, probably returning to class from getting a drink of water, when two girls approached me.

"Aundrea, do you want to be white?" one of the girls asked. I paused for a moment and responded with an awkward "no," and kept walking. "Well, all of your friends are white," she hollered at me. I put my head down and continued to walk back to my fourth grade classroom. I did not know how to feel at the moment. I did not understand where her comment came from. Honestly, I do not think I thought about skin color before that day. Yes, I knew I was black. Yes, I knew that some of my friends were not. But what I did not realize was that it mattered.

That day was the first time I realized that to some, in order to be black, you had to fit a certain mold, and whom I chose to be friends with was important to some people. Before that day I was just being Aundrea. Before that day I was just living my little nine-year-old life. Before that day I was listening to New Kids on the Block and Boyz II Men trying to figure out which one would be my boyfriend for the day. The comment shifted my thinking. Her words definitely hit a nerve. This girl continued to taunt me throughout my fourth- and fifth-grade years. She made sly comments about me to her friends and threatened to jump me several times. I was scared and tried to avoid her at all costs. This interaction did not result in me distancing myself from my friends, but it made me aware. It woke me up. At the end of my fifth-grade year, I said goodbye to my friends and broke the news to them that I would not be joining them in middle school. Interestingly enough I wasn't sad. I was relieved. I knew I did not want to endure any more bullying. My parents had decided to enroll me in Catholic school. I now had to start over. I had to make new friends. I wondered if whom I hung out with in this new space would matter to my new classmates.

CHAPTER 5

"SHINE MY SHOES, SLAVE GIRL"

In the sixth and seventh grades, I was one of two black students in middle school (the other student was mixed—black and white). It was a very small school, which I think made me stand out even more as an "outsider." When I arrived, I realized that I did not get the memo that my skirt needed to be just below my crotch. Mine was basically at my ankles (Thanks, mom). Red vest, white collared skirt, and a plaid kilt. This combination made it almost impossible to roll up my skirt. My shirt had to be tucked in, so there was no place to hide the fifteen rolls I would have had to create to achieve a more "acceptable" look. Most of the students were friendly and my blackness wasn't questioned, however, I was called a slave girl and asked to shine a few shoes.

I was just having a normal conversation with a classmate and I must have said something that the boy didn't like. "Yeah, okay slave girl. Why don't you get down here and shine my shoes?" he retorted. *Did anyone else hear that?* I thought to myself. The hallway was filled with students on their way to their next class. Someone must have heard that, right? I think I may have responded with a sarcastic comment about him being short, but I may have only said that loud enough for me to hear. I had no clue what to say. I heard about black people being spoken to that way, but I never thought I would be on the receiving end. Some of the students also compared their pigment to mine when they returned from the beach. "Aundrea, I'm almost as dark as you," they would say. I recall sitting down for class and someone behind me asked, "What kind of name is Aundrea anyway?" I was being harassed for two things that were out of my control. Being black and the pronunciation of my name, ON-DREE-AH.

It's still so interesting to me that children can identify what society has deemed as a weakness and pick at it, not realizing the impact their comments may have on the social-emotional well-being of the recipient. Or maybe our culture has created a world where kids know it's wrong, but they are taught not to care. I'm not sure. I've worked with kids for more than half of my life and the question I ask myself every single year is, *Why are kids so mean to each other?*

I never had an issue with getting good grades. I felt I was good at all subjects until a pivotal moment in my seventh grade math class. The teacher asked the class to solve a problem in our notebooks that she put up on the chalkboard. I was trying my hardest to solve it, but I did not understand the concept. I gave up and as soon as I put my pencil down in defeat the teacher called on me. "I don't know how to do this," I said. She didn't respond. She just stared at me. We must've been sitting in silence for about five minutes. I slowly took out my glasses and placed them on my face, even though I could see the board perfectly fine from where I was sitting. "That's a smart move," one of the other students called out. Still the teacher said nothing. After a while, her face started to twist up in anger, but instead of giving me some strategies to break down the problem, she said, "Come on, this is one of the easy ones. How do you not know the answer?" A pit started to form in my stomach. I still had no clue. Eventually she gave up on me and called on someone else who was able to solve it in about 2.5 seconds. When the student was finished, the teacher turned and deviously looked at me. I sunk down in my chair praying the class would be over soon. I don't know why the teacher reacted that way towards me. Could she have just been an awful teacher who liked to see her students squirm uncomfortably in their seats? It's possible, but with the way things had been going I could only attribute it to one thing: she did not like me. And she did not like me because I was black. I do not know this to be 100% true, but that's how she made me feel.

CHAPTER 6

LISPTICK AND LIES

Needless to say, during a time when you begin to like boys and have "boyfriends," I was left alone. The boys at school weren't checking for me, and when the black boys from the local public school would come to our school events or just hang out outside after dismissal, they wanted nothing to do with me. I tried putting on lipstick for the first time in hopes that it would make me more attractive. It didn't. My mom picked me up from school that day and, feeling defeated, I slowly got into the passenger seat of her car. I forgot that I had on the lipstick until my mom said, "Aundrea, what's on your mouth?" *Oh crap!* "Uhhh, nothing," I replied. Without saying a word, my mom handed me a tissue. I knew exactly what she wanted me to do. I gently wiped my lips, hopeful that if I wiped lightly enough nothing would show up on the tissue. I was wrong. A bright pink smudge spread across the white tissue. "You don't need to wear lipstick to impress those stupid boys," she said, "And you don't need to lie to me either."

There was one stupid boy, however, that I felt the need to impress. I had the biggest crush on him, Danny S. (I know his full last name, but I will spare him the embarrassment). I talked about him all the time and every time he walked into the gym I would freeze up. I think he went to Port Chester High School. One day after a boys' basketball game, a group of us were hanging out in the gym. I don't know what came over me, but I just walked over and talked to him. "I know you don't know me, but I know you. I think you're cute and I would like to hang out with you sometime." I was shaking. He just nodded his head up and down and said, "Oooookaaaaay?" I then turned and swiftly walked away. "Who's that black girl anyway?" I heard him ask his friend. I knew he liked the head cheerleader, who was white, but I thought I would take the chance anyway. Mind you, he was also black. The funny part is after I said my spiel I no longer was interested. It was as if I just needed to get my thoughts out to be able to move on. I actually ended up seeing him three or four years later walking near the local mall. I said nothing nor did I feel the need to. He probably wouldn't have remembered me anyway.

CHAPTER 7

JUST A SKINNY BLACK GIRL

Ironically, although I was surrounded by the European standard of beauty in school, I had no desire to be white. My involvement in things outside of my school community created a sense of pride in being black. But with that pride came a realization that I did not "fit in" with the people of my culture, yet again. I think a large part of that had to do with the fact that some of the black folk around me made me feel that not only did being quiet and having white friends make me weak or invisible, but so did having a slim frame. They felt they could say or do whatever they wanted to me because I would not defend myself. I started to believe them. Being the skinny black chick was something else that (I thought) pushed me further away from "being black." I actually prayed for wider hips and a bigger butt. Clearly that didn't happen, but I was tired of being the scrawny one. "Girl, you need to eat a sandwich," they would tell me. *But I just ate two*, I would think to myself.

Isn't it enough that the world judges us so harshly? Why do we have to be so hard on each other? The power and love that could radiate from all black and brown women if we just took the time to love ourselves and love our black and brown sisters would be world-changing. If every healthy and positive image that was put out into the world of a woman of color was praised and celebrated, instead of picked apart, we would be in a much different headspace. There are many positive outlets available for women of color to see, connect with, and engage with other women who look like us. I am so happy they exist now, especially for my son and my daughter to witness, but I wish I had something to hold on to when I was a kid. Don't get me wrong, I had positive, powerful, and beautiful women of color in my life, but when you are surrounded by people who do not look like you in school and in the media, what's "acceptable" and "not acceptable" begin to blur—and not just for white people, but for black people too.

This became my normal. Of course, looking back, I realize that this was not normal, but at eleven and twelve years old, I learned to normalize situations in order to cope. I was so taken aback by the comments that I was unable to fully process the severity of the words and actions that were used, so I pushed them to the side and moved on faster than I should have. My mom's face when I told her what I was experiencing is still fresh in my mind. I was not able to go into detail with her about my body image issues. I think I was too young and too hurt to fully articulate how I felt about my physique, but she knew that I wore two pairs of slouch socks because I thought if my ankles were covered my legs wouldn't look so skinny.

I do not know what my mom said or to whom at my school she addressed, but I know she gave them a piece of her mind. I ended up transferring schools after two years. By the time my classmates threw a surprise going-away party for me, my main tormenter, the one who taunted me with racist comments, was actually someone I called a "friend". I know. Crazy. I wish I had known the words to use when discriminatory comments were thrown at me, but that's not something that you think you need to prepare yourself for in the seventh grade. It would have been different if I wasn't the only one being taunted in that way, but I was. I had no one to talk to about this at school. So, let's think about this. As children we are in school for about eight hours a day. That's about forty hours a week. So if we count the comments made outside of school and the comments made while in school, I spent forty-plus hours a week unsure of how to stand up for myself. I spent forty-plus hours a week trying to find my voice and I failed. A subconscious feeling of loneliness set in. I smiled and laughed, but when there is no one else like you, no one else to trade stories with, no one else experiencing the same ridicule and racism, the emptiness begins to grow. I began to think that my voice was not strong enough to handle life.

CHAPTER 8

DÉJÀ VU

My eighth-grade year introduced me to new friends, real friends, friends of color, some of whom I still speak with today. Interestingly enough, it was one of those middle school friends who made an innocent observation about how my words flowed. The way I spoke caused her to make a statement that made me pause and ponder her words, yet again unsure of how to respond. We were laughing and joking, heading down the hill to recess, when she said with a chuckle, "Aundrea, you talk so white." I honestly do not remember my response, I probably just laughed it off, like always, but the statement stung. It stuck. *What does that mean? What do you mean I talk white? And why do people keep saying things like this to me?* Granted, we were young and it wasn't done to be cruel, but I felt like I was reliving moments in my life that caused me so much pain.

I remember sitting on a train with my sister, having a conversation with one of the other passengers, and when we were done speaking, he leaned over to his friend and asked him, "Doesn't she sound like a white girl?" I honestly did not know who I was anymore. I had black people telling me I didn't hang out with them enough, talk like them, or look like them (and I needed to do something about it) and I had white people ridiculing me for simply being me. I started to second-guess every single word that left my mouth. I didn't want to say something that would result in another jab or insult. I just smiled and laughed it away, again. The stage had been set. I now believed what others thought and said about me. I chose to believe such opposite ends of the spectrum (the white perspective of me and black perspective of me), which resulted in me fading away. Well, if you think about it, they really weren't on opposite ends; both parties were telling me that who I was wasn't good enough. I mentioned earlier that because of the color of our skin, our experiences as black women are pre-determined. Being a black girl in these scenarios seems to have triggered something in others that made them feel as though they needed to break me down. Instead of folks just accepting me and appreciating me for what I had to offer, I was consistently blind-sided with judgment. I hate to think about all of the little black girls who are going through this as I write because even with the positive outlets that exist, the self-worth of our black and brown children is still low.

CHAPTER 9

"MAYBE NEXT TIME"

I attended two different high schools, and in both institutions was one of the few black students. I remember being immediately greeted by an amazing individual on my first day of eleventh grade. This was the first time in a long time that no one questioned how I spoke or my skinny frame. I was introduced to the other black and brown students in my class and brought to the table where people who looked like us sat. That in itself is telling, right? We had our own table. We needed to create a space where we felt comfortable enough to be ourselves. Although there was clearly an unspoken racial divide, it was there that I truly began to push myself to move to the next level in my studies. I even went so far as to have a conversation with my English teacher and ask her if I could take the AP English exam. She hesitated when I asked the question. At the time I could not pinpoint what led to her slow response, but she eventually said she would let me know when the exam was taking place. A few days later, as I sat in one of my other classes, I noticed a few students arriving late. "Where are you all coming from?" I asked.

"Oh, we just finished taking the AP English exam," one of the girls responded.

I clearly had not been informed of the date of the exam. When I asked my teacher why she did not let me know when the exam was, she calmly stated, "I didn't think you were quite ready yet." "But I have been getting all A's in your class," I replied. "Really? Well, maybe next time," she said. Yeah, maybe next time. I really thought this teacher had my back, but clearly I was wrong. Now don't get me wrong, I had great teachers here and have amazing memories of the things I learned and the people I met, but I kept running into a wall. A wall that I did not know existed until my face lay squished against the bricks.

CHAPTER 10

IS IT WORTH IT?

Something that I struggle with even to this day is whether or not it is worth being the only person of color in the room if it is said the circumstances will lead to a "better" education. I just don't know if it is. I know there are kids out there who have experienced what I went through times ten. I know there are parents, like my parents, who just want to make sure their child is getting everything that they can out of their educational experience. However, my years of teaching has shown me that a child's social-emotional stability needs to be intact in order for them to thrive academically. If I had been able to speak to someone at school who may have been experiencing the same thing that I was, or maybe if there was more of us, I would not have experienced the torment and overwhelming self-doubt at all. I see the effect on the black and brown students that I have come into contact with throughout the years. Students who have been the only child of color in their class since kindergarten. Students whose hair is continuously pet, students whose economic status is assumed to be lower class, students who are spoken to like they don't matter.

On the flip side, after some children have spent the entire day just trying to figure out how to fit in, they now must go home (and by home I mean church, their neighborhood, a family gathering, etc.), and encounter ridicule for being in a white space. Those children essentially have to be two different people. How do they know how to be themselves? There is a stigma that follows a black child who attends a predominately white school, or in my case, has white friends. Some people in the black community feel like that family thinks they are better than them. "What, you think you are too good to go our school?" some may ask. Maybe the better question is, why is there such a disparity in the quality of education kids receive when there is a higher population of kids of color?

CHAPTER 11

AWAKE

It was now time for me to decide where I wanted to go for college. I chose Temple University. It was far enough away from home for independence, but close enough to go back home if I got homesick. Although, to an outsider, Temple may appear to have a large number of students of color, it actually does not. What's funny is that, much like in high school, we all managed to find each other at the same table.

I was not an outgoing freshman. I kept to myself. This was a new space. I had to figure out if I fit in here. During one of the orientation events, a girl told me that I needed to talk more. I just smiled back. My old insecurities began to set in again. I became so hyperaware of how I thought others perceived me, especially people of color, that I reverted back to my middle school mind-set. *Just smile and nod, Aundrea. Just smile and nod.* However, I was able to make some really good friends. It's so interesting that I did not realize until writing this that throughout my life, even during the most difficult times, there were people in my life that had my back. God is truly amazing. The friends that I made in college did not mind my awkward black girl presence. I made friends who were the total opposite of me. They were loud, out-going, and honest. Fifteen-plus years later and we are still friends. And yes, they are all black.

It was at Temple that I went natural, and by natural I mean I decided not to put chemicals in my hair to maintain its straight appearance. When I decided not to get a relaxer anymore, I honestly just wanted to see what my hair would do. I did not care what anyone else thought about me. I was there to learn. Period. Yes, I did look a hot mess at times. Going natural on a college budget is rough, but I hung in there. There was a point during my transition phase that I did not realize (or was in denial about) that my hair texture had changed. I wanted to protect my hair so I went and got a weave with "minimum leave out." I found someone who would do it for a reasonable price. Bad idea. I spent so much time trying to smooth out the hair that was "left out", trying relentlessly to remove the natural curl pattern my hair had started to form that peeked out of the weave, that I am sure I singed the top of my head.

I honestly think that going natural was one of the best things I have ever done in my life. When I decided to make this change, I was feeling very comfortable and confident in who I was. I had come a long way. I was more comfortable speaking my mind, say-ing no, and not following the crowd. For me, this hair transition was the icing on the cake. I was proclaiming to the world, "Take me as I am, and if you don't, I don't need you anyway."

It was at Temple that I was able to take a course in African-American studies, Yoruba religion, and various dialects and vernaculars. It was there that I was around black people who came in all shapes and sizes, who spoke a variety of dialects, and who did not judge me for mine. It was there that I began to understand why folks felt the need to question how I spoke. In one of my classes a label was finally placed on how I spoke. I am a black woman who speaks Standard English. Also known as "talking white" or "speaking intelligently." My upbringing, my experiences all contributed to this. It was not something I tried to do; it was something that was just me.

My life experiences also taught me how to code-switch and how to play the game. My childhood and high school experiences in a predominantly white space, allowed me to understand how to navigate being one of a handful of black people at work. However, although I have a very good reputation at the institution where I currently work, and have been working there for twelve years, I find myself not wanting to play the game anymore. I no longer want to be the "token." And by token I mean the black girl who sits back, smiles, and does what she is told even if it is against her beliefs and values. I want to make a change. I find myself speaking out more about the subtle and not so subtle nuances that are affecting the students of color. I do not want a little black child in this predominantly white environment to ever feel like his or her voice was not strong enough to handle life. I have made it my mission to make sure the black and brown students see me in a positive light and recognize that I am a leader in the community and my voice has power and their voices do, too. The very thing people questioned me about growing up is the very thing that has shaped me into the creator, daughter, sister, wife, mother, Christian, and black woman that I am today. It's the very thing that I love about myself and others love about me. Who you are, is who you are. The opinions, judgments, or criticisms of others do not define you.

EPILOGUE

SPEAK YOUR TRUTH

For the Quiet Black Girl... was written to reach the little girl who does not quite know where she fits in. I created this book for the black woman who may still be struggling to find her voice after all of those years of suppressing it. I wrote this book to encourage you, the reader, and to let you know that you are not alone, and your voice does matter. I also wrote this book to let you know what I would have done differently. If I could go back to that moment in elementary school when I was asked if I wanted to be white, to that moment when I was called a slave girl in middle school, to that moment when my high school English teacher "didn't think I was ready," I would reach down into the depths of my soul and find my voice. I would scream, "No I don't want to be white! Do you think that just because I have white friends I am not proud of who I am?" And to the boy who called me a slave girl, "What the hell is wrong with you? Don't you EVER refer to me as a slave girl again." And to my English teacher, "I should have been given the opportunity to take the exam. You didn't have the right to make that decision for me. I work extremely hard in this class and I have the right to take that test."

I also regret not confiding in my mom more. Naturally I am an introvert, but I wish I didn't take it all on by myself. At the time, I just smiled and tried to shake off what I was feeling. But all of those emotions are too much for a child to bear alone. But I did not know how to use my voice. I did not know the power it had. I allowed fear to take over every ounce of my being, but you don't have to do that. There is a quote that I love and hold dear. It is from Maggie Kuhn, an American social activist who was central in establishing the group that became known as the Gray Panthers, which works for the rights and welfare of the elderly. She says: "Leave safety behind. Put your body on the line. Stand before the people you fear and speak your mind—even if your voice shakes. When you least expect it, someone may actually listen to what you have to say. Well-aimed slingshots can topple giants." Even if your voice shakes, my dear, SPEAK YOUR TRUTH.

The late great W.E.B Dubois, a leading African-American sociologist, writer, activist, and a founding officer of the National Association for the Advancement of Colored People (NAACP) wrote,

"One ever feels his twoness,—an American, a Negro; two souls, two thoughts, two unreconciled strivings; two warring ideals in one dark body, whose strength alone keeps it from being torn asunder."

There are no other words that I could write that fully describe what I have felt all of these years. This quote from W.E.B Dubois's *The Souls of Black Folk* hit me at my core. His words allowed me to see myself. They gave me a mirror, not to see my physical reflection, but to see my experiences and hear my innermost thoughts. If you do not have a mirror, one that allows you to live your truth, someone in your space who you can relate to and honestly share your challenges and successes with, it is so important that you find one. You may need to look to organizations that are not part of your school or work community to do this, and that is okay. But please, I beg you, never feel like you do not belong here. *Never feel like you do not belong here.* You are beautiful. You are strong. You matter, so speak your truth—even if your voice shakes.

Made in the USA
Middletown, DE
26 September 2018